George Harrison

Biography Of The Brilliant Beatles' Guitarist

By

Amanda Geraldine

George Harrison

Table Of Contents

George Harrison

<u>PREFACE</u>

George Harrison MBE, an English musician, and singer-songwriter who died on November 29, 2001, rose to prominence around the world as the Beatles' lead guitarist. Harrison, who was sometimes referred to as "the quiet Beatle," loved Indian culture and contributed to the expansion of popular music by incorporating Indian instruments and spirituality that were in line with Hinduism. The majority of Beatles albums from 1965 onwards included at least two Harrison compositions, even though John Lennon and Paul McCartney wrote the majority of the band's songs. "Taxman," "Within You Without You," "While My Guitar Gently Weeps," "Here Comes the Sun," and "Something" are some of the songs he wrote for the band. Early musical influences on Harrison included Django Reinhardt and George Formby, followed by Carl Perkins, Chet Atkins, and Chuck Berry.

By 1965, he had started to guide the Beatles toward Indian classical music through his use of Indian instruments like the sitar, which he had learned to play on the Help! set, and into folk rock through his interest in Bob Dylan and the Byrds. From "Norwegian Wood (This Bird Has Flown)" onward, he contributed sitar to many Beatles songs.

He was the driving force behind the band's adoption of Transcendental Meditation in 1967 and later became associated with the Hare Krishna movement. Harrison's triple album All Things Must Pass, which received critical praise after the band disbanded in 1970, featured his most popular hit song, "My Sweet

Lord," as well as the slide guitar, which would become his trademark sound as a solo performer. Along with Indian musician Ravi Shankar, he also organized the Concert for Bangladesh in 1971, which served as a model for later charity events like Live Aid. Harrison worked as a record producer for artists signed to the Beatles' Apple label before starting Dark Horse Records in 1974. Harrison also co-founded HandMade Films in 1978, initially intending to produce the Monty Python movie The Life of Brian (1979).

As a solo artist, Harrison put out several top-selling songs and albums. He created the platinum-selling supergroup the Traveling Wilburys with them in 1988. He was a prolific recording artist who worked with artists like Dylan, Eric Clapton, Ringo Starr, and Tom

Petty on songs and music. He also appeared as a guest guitarist on songs by Badfinger, Ronnie Wood, and Billy Preston. He was voted 11th among the "100 Greatest Guitarists of All Time" by Rolling Stone magazine. He was twice inducted into the Rock & Roll Hall of Fame: once posthumously for his solo career in 2004 and once as a member of the Beatles in 1988.

The first marriage Harrison had, to model Pattie Boyd, ended in divorce in 1977. He married Olivia Arias the next year, and the two were blessed with a son named Dhani. At the age of 58 and two years after escaping a knife attack by an intruder at his house, Friar Park, Harrison passed away from lung cancer in 2001. His body was cremated, and the ashes were dispersed in a private Hindu ceremony in

India's Ganges and Yamuna rivers. His estate was close to £100 million.

<u>1943–1958: CHILDHOOD</u>

On February 25, 1943, Harrison was born in Wavertree, Liverpool, at 12 Arnold Grove. He was the youngest of Harold Hargreaves (or Hargrove) Harrison's (born French; 1911–1970) four children. Louise was an Irish Catholic shop assistant, and Harold was a bus conductor who had previously served as a ship's steward for the White Star Line. He had two brothers, Harold (born in 1934) and Peter (20 July 1940 - 1 June 2007), as well as one sister, Louise (16 August 1931 - 29 January 2023).

Harrison's mother, according to Boyd, was especially encouraging: "All she wanted for her children was to be happy, and she recognized that nothing made George quite as happy as making music."

Louise was a passionate music lover, and among her friends, she was renowned for her strong singing voice, which occasionally shocked guests by rattling the Harrisons' windows. Louise frequently listened to the weekly transmission of Radio India while she was carrying George. According to Joshua Greene, who wrote a biography of Harrison, "Every Sunday she tuned in to mystical sounds evoked by sitars and tablas, hoping that the exotic music would bring peace and calm to the baby in the womb."

Harrison spent the first four years of his childhood in a terraced home on a cul-de-sac at 12 Arnold Grove. The only source of heat in the house was a single coal stove, and it had an outdoor toilet. The family relocated to 25 Upton Green in Speke after accepting a council housing offer in 1949. Harrison started attending Dovedale Primary School in 1948 when he was five years old. He attended Liverpool Institute High School for Boys from 1954 to 1959 after passing the eleven-plus test. Harrison was dissatisfied with the lack of guitars in the institution's music classes, and he believed that the school "molded students into being frightened" even though the institute did provide a music course.

Early musical influences on Harrison included Hoagy Carmichael, George Formby, Cab Calloway, and Django Reinhardt; by the 1950s, Carl Perkins and Lonnie Donegan had become important figures.

He had a lightbulb moment in the early months of 1956 when he heard Elvis Presley's "Heartbreak Hotel" being played from a nearby house, sparking his interest in rock and roll. He would often sketch guitars in his school books while sitting at the back of the room, saying afterward, "I was totally into guitars." Another early inspiration mentioned by Harrison was Slim Whitman:

The first person I ever saw playing the guitar, either a snapshot of him in a magazine or live on television was Slim Whitman. Guitars were undoubtedly arriving.
–He claimed.

Harold Harrison initially had doubts about his son's desire to pursue a music career. However, according to Harold, he spent £3.10s.- (or £90 in 2023) on a Dutch Egmond flat-top acoustic guitar in 1956 to buy a George one. Harrison learned how to play "Whispering," "Sweet Sue," and "Dinah" from one of his father's friends. Harrison, his brother Peter, and a friend named Arthur Kelly started a skiffle band called the Rebels after being influenced by Donegan's music.

Paul McCartney, who attended the Liverpool Institute, and Harrison connected over their common love of music while riding the school bus to their respective campuses.

<u>1958–1970: CAREER WITH THE BEATLES</u>

McCartney and John Lennon were members of the Quarrymen, a skiffle outfit. Harrison performed the "Guitar Boogie Shuffle" by Arthur "Guitar Boogie" Smith during an audition for the Quarrymen in Rory Storm's Morgue Skiffle Club in March 1958 at McCartney's suggestion. Lennon rejected Harrison because he had only turned 15 at the time. In a second meeting that McCartney set up, Harrison dazzled Lennon by playing the lead guitar part for the instrumental "Raunchy" on the upper deck of a bus in Liverpool. He started interacting with the group and stepping in to play guitar as needed before being welcomed as a member. Harrison dropped out of school at the age of 16, against his father's wishes for him to pursue his studies, and spent several months working as an apprentice electrician at a nearby department store, Blacklers. Harrison referred to Carl Perkins by the moniker "Carl Harrison" during the band's first trip to Scotland in 1960.

The group, now going by the name of the Beatles, was scheduled to perform in 1960 at Bruno Koschmider S Indra and Kaiserkeller clubs in Hamburg. The first time they lived in Hamburg, Harrison was deported because he was too young to work in nightclubs, which brought an early end to their stay. They had their image polished when Brian Epstein took over as their manager in December 1961, and he later got them an EMI recording deal. When the group's debut album, Please Please Me, was released in early 1963, Beatlemania had already begun. The group's first song, "Love Me Do," peaked at number 17 on the Record Retailer chart. Harrison was referred to as "the quiet Beatle" since he was frequently somber and concentrated on stage with the band.

Harrison was diagnosed with Strep throat, ran a fever, and was told by doctors to refrain from speaking until he made his scheduled appearance on The Ed Sullivan Show in early 1964. At that time, the Beatles had just arrived in the country. As a result, the label persisted, much to Harrison's amusement, after the press noticed his apparent laconic demeanor throughout public appearances on that tour. In addition to three lead vocal credits on their second album, With the Beatles (1963), he also got two lead vocal credits on the LP, which included the Lennon-McCartney song "Do You

Want to Know a Secret?" The latter contained Harrison's debut solo composition, "Don't Bother Me."

Harrison, who was particularly versed in soul music, functioned as the Beatles' scout for fresh American albums. He started to influence the other Beatles' musical tastes with 1965's Rubber Soul, introducing them to folk rock through his love of the Byrds and Bob Dylan, as well as Indian classical music with his usage of the sitar on "Norwegian Wood (This Bird Has Flown)". He afterward referred to Rubber Soul as his "favorite Beatles album." Three of his works were on Revolver (1966): "Taxman," chosen as the album's first track, "Love You To," and "I Want to Tell You." His drone-like tambura portion on Lennon's "Tomorrow Never Knows" highlighted the band's continued investigation of non-Western instruments, while the sitar- and tabla-based "Love You To" signified the Beatles' first sincere dive into Indian music. The latter song established a precedent in popular music as an instance of Asian culture being represented by Westerners respectfully and without mockery, claims ethnomusicologist David Reck. Harrison gained notoriety as "the maharaja of raga-rock" after "Norwegian Wood" due to his increased sitar use, according to author Nicholas Schaffner's 1978 essay.

Harrison used "Strawberry Fields Forever" to further explore his fascination with non-Western instruments by playing swarmandal.

Harrison's interests had shifted away from the Beatles by late 1966. He chose Eastern gurus and religious figures to appear on the album cover of Sgt. Pepper's Lonely Hearts Club Band in 1967. The "Within You Without You" song, which was inspired by Indian music, was his only original creation on the album. No other Beatle helped with it. On the song, he performed sitar and tambura with support from the London Asian Music Circle's dilruba, swarmandal, and tabla players. The Sgt. Pepper album, he subsequently said, "was a millstone and a milestone in the music industry... About half of the songs I listen to are ones I like, and the other half I detest."

At the EMI studio in Bombay in January 1968, he cut the basic track for his song "The Inner Light" using a group of neighborhood musicians playing traditional Indian instruments. It served as the B-side to

McCartney's "Lady Madonna" and was the first Harrison song to be featured on a Beatles single. The song's lyrics, which were taken from a passage in the Tao Te Ching, reflected Harrison's growing interest in Hinduism and meditation. Ringo Starr briefly left the band as a result of internal strife that arose during The Beatles' recording the same year. While "My Guitar Gently Weeps" and the horn-driven "Savoy Truffle" were two of Harrison's four songwriting contributions to the double album. Lead guitar on "While My Guitar Gently Weeps" was played by Eric Clapton.

At the end of his time with the Beatles, Harrison was greatly influenced musically by Dylan and the Band. He made a friendship with Dylan at Woodstock in late 1968 and was drawn to the Band's sense of collaborative music-making and the members' equal creative freedom, which contrasted with Lennon and McCartney's dominance of the Beatles' songwriting and artistic direction. This was at the same time when his songwriting was at its peak and his desire to distance himself from the Beatles was rising. The group's conflicts reemerged in January 1969 at Twickenham Studios during the rehearsals that were captured on film and later turned into the 1970 documentary Let It Be. Harrison left the Beatles on January 10 due to his frustration with the icy and sterile film studio, Lennon's creative disengagement from the band, and what he saw as McCartney's authoritarian demeanor. After his bandmates had decided to move the film project to their own Apple Studio and drop McCartney's plan to resume live performances, he came back 12 days later.

When the Beatles recorded their 1969 album
Abbey Road, things were less tense but still far
from perfect. Harrison's "two classic
contributions" to the album—"Here Comes the
Sun" and "Something"—helped him "finally
achieve equal songwriting status" with Lennon
and McCartney. Harrison exercised greater
creative control during the album's recording,
rejecting McCartney's and other musicians'
recommendations for alterations to his work.

When "Something" and "Come Together" was
released as a double A-side single, it became his
first A-side; the song reached number one in
Canada, Australia, West Germany, and New
Zealand, while the record's combined sides
peaked at number one on the Billboard Hot 100
chart in the United States. Frank Sinatra twice
recorded "Something" in the 1970s (1970 and

1979), referring to it as "the greatest love song of the past fifty years" in a later interview. It was regarded as the best song on Abbey Road by John Lennon, and it overtook "Yesterday" as the Beatles' second most frequently covered song.

Harrison's song "For You Blue" and McCartney's "The Long and Winding Road" were combined on a US single in May 1970, and the single became Harrison's second chart-topper when both sides were ranked at the top of the Hot 100. By the time of their breakup, he had amassed a collection of unpublished compositions thanks to his increased productivity. Harrison's growing skill as a songwriter was frustrated by the fact that only two or three songs from his compositions appeared on Beatles albums, which greatly contributed to the band's dissolution. On January 4, 1970, Harrison, McCartney, and Starr recorded his song "I Me Mine" for the Let It Be soundtrack album, marking his final recording session with the Beatles.

1968–1987: SOLO CAREER

1968–1969: First Solo Projects

Harrison had previously created and published two solo albums before the breakup of the Beatles: Wonderwall Music and Electronic Sound, both of which are composed primarily of instrumental music. Indian and Western instruments are combined on Wonderwall Music, the soundtrack to the 1968 movie Wonderwall, while a Moog synthesizer is extensively featured on Electronic Sound, an experimental record. Wonderwall Music was the first solo album by a Beatle and the first LP issued by Apple Records. It was released in November 1968. On the album, which features the experimental sound collage "Dream Scene," which was recorded several months before John

Lennon's "Revolution 9," Indian musicians Aashish Khan and Shivkumar Sharma contributed.

Harrison took part in a brief European tour in December 1969 with the American band Delaney & Bonnie and Friends. Harrison started playing slide guitar during the tour, which also featured Clapton, Bobby Whitlock, Jim Gordon on the drums, and band leaders Delaney and Bonnie Bramlett. He also started writing "My Sweet Lord," which would later become his debut song as a solo artist.

1970: All Things Must Pass

Harrison was unable to contribute songs to Beatles albums for a long time, but he eventually released All Things Must Pass, a triple album that had two CDs of his compositions and a third that featured recordings of Harrison improvising with pals. The record, which many considered to be his greatest, topped the charts on both sides of the Atlantic. The album, co-produced by Phil Spector using his "Wall of Sound" method, featured musicians such as Starr, Clapton, Gary Wright, Billy Preston, Klaus Voormann, the entirety of Delaney and Bonnie's Friends band, and the Apple group Badfinger. The top-ten single "What Is Life" and the number-one hit single "My Sweet Lord" were both taken from the album.

All Things Must Pass was well-received by critics upon release; Rolling Stone's Ben Gerson praised it as "music of mountain tops and vast horizons, of classic Spectorian proportions, Wagnerian, Brucknerian." The lyrics of the album's title tune, according to author and musicologist Ian Inglis, are "a recognition of the impermanence of human existence... a simple and poignant conclusion" to Harrison's previous band.

Because "My Sweet Lord" and the 1963 Chiffons hit song "He's So Fine" are so similar, Bright Tunes filed a lawsuit against Harrison for copyright infringement in 1971. He denied intentionally copying the song when the matter was heard in a US district court in 1976, but he lost because the judge determined that he had done it unintentionally.

Harrison enthusiastically promoted the album's thirty-fifth-anniversary version, which Apple Records issued in 2000. He discussed the work in an interview, saying, "It's just something that was like my continuation from the Beatles. It was a very happy occasion where I sort of left the Beatles and just went my own way." "Well, those days it was like the reverb was kind of used a bit more than what I would do now," he said in response to the production. "In actuality, I seldom ever employ reverb. I find it intolerable. It's challenging to revisit something thirty years later and expect it to still be in the same condition."

<u>1971: The Concert For Bangladesh</u>

In response to a request from Ravi Shankar, Harrison planned the Concert for Bangladesh, a charity concert that took place on August 1 of that year. Over 40,000 people attended the event's two performances at Madison Square Garden in New York. Fundraising for malnourished refugees during the Bangladesh Liberation War was the event's main objective. The performance, which included well-known musicians like Dylan, Clapton, Leon Russell, Badfinger, Preston, and Starr, was opened by Shankar.

The Concert for Bangladesh, a triple album, was released by Apple in December. A concert movie was also released in 1972. The album, which bears the "George Harrison and Friends" credit, was the number-one album in the UK and reached its peak at number two in the US. It later won the Grammy Award for Album of the Year. Many of the proceeds were later tied down by tax issues and dubious expenditures, but Harrison noted: "Mainly the concert was to draw attention to the situation... Although we had some financial difficulties, they still received plenty of the money we raised, even though it was only a drop in the ocean. The key thing was that we informed people and contributed to the conclusion of the war.

1973–1979: George Harrison's Experience Of The Material World

For five weeks in 1973, Harrison's album Living in the Material World topped the Billboard Albums chart, and the album's lead track "Give Me Love (Give Me Peace on Earth)" also peaked at the top of the US charts. The song debuted at number eight, and the album peaked at number two in the UK. Harrison's Hindu beliefs were the main theme of the beautifully constructed and packed album. It contained many of the strongest compositions of his career. In a Rolling Stone article, Stephen Holden praised the album as being "vastly appealing," "profoundly seductive," and "standing alone as an article of faith, miraculous in its radiance." The release was criticized by several reviews as uncomfortable, pompous, and too sentimental.

When Harrison launched his 45-date Dark Horse Tour in November 1974, he made history as the first ex-Beatle to tour North America. Billy Preston and Tom Scott from his band made guest appearances, and "Ravi Shankar, Family, and Friends" performed both traditional and modern Indian music during the performances. The tour received a lot of great reviews, but overall, people didn't like it. Many fans were offended by what Inglis referred to as Harrison's "sermonizing" and some found Shankar's significant presence to be an odd disappointment. Additionally, he changed the lyrics to several Beatles songs, and some critics referred to the tour as "dark hoarse" due to his laryngitis-related vocal problems. Although the Dark Horse tour may be viewed as a noble failure, some fans were paying attention to what was being attempted. They left thrilled, aware that what they had just seen was so inspiring that it could never happen again. The tour was dubbed "groundbreaking" and "revolutionary in its presentation of Indian Music" by Simon Leng.

Harrison's album Dark Horse, which he released in December, received the unfavorable reviews of his career. It was described as "the chronicle of a performer out of his element, working to a deadline, enfeebling his overtaxed talents by a rush to deliver a new 'LP product', rehearse a band, and assemble a cross-country tour, all within three weeks" by Rolling Stone. The single "Dark Horse" and the album both peaked at number 15 on the Billboard chart, although not one of them was successful in the UK. Dark Horse was dubbed "one of Harrison's most fascinating works - a record about change and loss" by music reviewer Mikal Gilmore.

The soul music-inspired Extra Texture (Read All About It) (1975), Harrison's final studio album for EMI and Apple Records, reached number 8 on the Billboard chart and number 16 in the UK. Since All Things Must Pass, Harrison had recorded three albums, and he thought this was the least satisfying of those. Leng noted "bitterness and dismay" in a number of the songs, and his lifelong friend Klaus Voormann said: "He wasn't up for it... I believe there was a lot of cocaine around at the time, which is when I left the relationship because I didn't like his mentality. In addition to "You," which peaked at number 20 on the Billboard Hot 100, he also released "This Guitar

(Can't Keep from Crying)," Apple's last original single release.

Harrison's debut studio album on his own Dark Horse Records label, Thirty-Three & 1/3 (1976), delivered the top 25 US singles "This Song" and "Crackerbox Palace." The absurd humor of "Crackerbox Palace" was a reflection of Harrison's friendship with Eric Idle of Monty Python, who also created the song's humorous music video. Harrison received his most positive reviews from US critics since All Things Must Pass with Thirty-Three & 1/3, which placed a strong focus on melody and musicianship and had a more nuanced message than his earlier efforts. The album outsold his two prior studio albums, however, its high there was well outside the top ten. Harrison appeared alongside Paul Simon on Saturday Night Live to play as part of his release promotion.

Harrison's second marriage and the birth of his son Dhani were followed by the publication of George Harrison in 1979. The album and the single "Blow Away" both made the Billboard Top 20 and were co-produced by Russ Titelman. With several of the tracks recorded in the serene backdrop of Maui in the Hawaiian archipelago, the album catalyzed Harrison's slow exit from the music industry. George Harrison was described by Leng as "melodic and lush... peaceful... the work of a man who had lived the rock and roll dream twice over and was now embracing domestic as well as spiritual bliss"

1980–1987: Somewhere In England To Cloud Nine

"While My Guitar Gently Weeps" by Harrison and Eric Clapton was performed during the 1987 Prince's Trust Concert in London.

Harrison was troubled by John Lennon's assassination on December 8, 1980, and it reaffirmed his long-standing worry about stalkers. Although Harrison and Lennon had little interaction in the years before Lennon's death, the tragedy also represented a profound personal loss for Harrison. Harrison said, "After all we went through together I had and still have great love and respect for John Lennon," in response to the assassination. Harrison changed the song's lyrics to make it an homage to Lennon after writing it for Starr. Paul and Linda McCartney contributed vocals to "All Those Years Ago," which also used Starr's original drum section, and it hit number two on the US charts. The single was released in 1981 and was a part of the album Somewhere in England.

After 1982's Gone Troppo received little attention from reviewers or the general public, Harrison did not release another album for five years. He performed many times as a guest during this time, including once in 1985 at a Carl Perkins homage called Blue Suede Shoes: A Rockabilly Session. He made an unexpected cameo at the Birmingham HeartBeat Charity Concert's finale in March 1986, which was held to raise money for the Birmingham Children's Hospital. He performed "While My Guitar Gently Weeps" and "Here Comes the Sun" at The Prince's Trust concert at London's

Wembley Arena the following year. He appeared on stage with Bob Dylan, John Fogerty, Jesse Ed Davis, and the Taj Mahal in February 1987 for a two-hour concert.

"Bob rang me up and asked if I wanted to come out for the evening and see the Taj Mahal," Harrison recalled. "We got there and consumed some of these Mexican beers, followed by some more." "Hey, why don't we all get up and start playing, and you can sing," says Bob. "But whenever I approached the microphone, Dylan would approach and just start singing nonsense in my ear, trying to frighten me."

Harrison released his platinum-certified album Cloud Nine in November 1987. Harrison's cover of James Ray's "Got My Mind Set on You" appeared on the album, which was co-produced by Jeff Lynne of the Electric Light Orchestra

(ELO) and reached the top spot in the US and the UK. The accompanying music video gained a lot of airtime, and another song, "When We Were Fab," which looked back on the career of the Beatles, garnered two nominations for MTV Music Video Awards in 1988. Harrison's slide guitar skills were extensively featured on the album, which was recorded at his Friar Park house and featured some of his longtime musical partners, including Clapton, Jim Keltner, and Jim Horn. On the US and UK charts, Cloud Nine peaked at number eight and number ten, respectively. "Devil's Radio," "This Is Love," and "Cloud 9" all made it onto the Billboard Mainstream Rock chart.

1988–1996: LATER CAREER

1988–1992: Return To Touring With The Traveling Wilburys

Harrison joined forces with Jeff Lynne, Roy Orbison, Bob Dylan, and Tom Petty to form the Traveling Wilburys in 1988. In Dylan's garage, the band had met to record a song for Harrison's next European single. The track "Handle with Care" was originally intended as a B-side, but Harrison's record company thought it was too wonderful for that and requested a complete album instead. The album, Traveling Wilburys Vol. 1, was published in October 1988. Half-brothers who were allegedly the sons of Charles Truscott Wilbury, Sr., were recorded under false names. In the US, where it was triple platinum certified, it peaked at number three and debuted at number 16 in the UK. Harrison adopted the alias "Nelson Wilbury" on the record; for their follow-up, he went by "Spike Wilbury."

Harrison and Starr made an appearance in Petty's "I Won't Back Down" music video in 1989. Harrison put together and published Best of Dark Horse 1976-1989, a collection of his later solo work, in October of that year. Three brand-new songs were featured on the CD, including "Cheer Down," which Harrison just wrote for the Lethal Weapon 2 soundtrack.

The Wilburys started recording as a four-piece when Orbison passed away in December 1988. The title of their second album, Traveling Wilburys Vol. 3, which was released in October

1990, was tongue-in-cheek. Lynne stated, "That was George's idea. 'Let's confuse the buggers,' he said. In the US, where it was certified platinum, it peaked at number 11, while it peaked at number 14 in the UK. Following the release of their second album, The Wilburys did not collaborate on any additional recordings. They also never gave a live performance.

Harrison accompanied Clapton on a tour of Japan in December 1991. Harrison hadn't released one since 1974, and none more did. Harrison gave his first London performance since the Beatles' 1969 rooftop concert at the Royal Albert Hall on April 6, 1992, during a charity performance for the Natural Law Party. He shared the stage with Dylan, Clapton, McGuinn, Tom Petty, and Neil Young at a

George Harrison

Madison Square Garden tribute event to Bob Dylan in October 1992.

<u>1994–1996 The Beatles Anthology</u>

Harrison started working on the Beatles Anthology project in 1994 alongside McCartney, Starr, and producer Jeff Lynne. This includes extensive interviews regarding the Beatles' history as well as the recording of two brand-new Beatles songs based on Lennon's solo vocal and piano tapes. The Beatles hadn't released a new single since 1970 until "Free as a Bird" was released in December 1995. The second single they released was "Real Love" in March 1996. Harrison steadfastly declined to take part in the creation of a third song. Later, he said of the endeavor, "I hope somebody does this to all my crap demos when I'm dead, makes them into hit songs."

1997-2001: LATER LIFE AND DEATH

Harrison and Ravi Shankar worked together on the latter's Chants of India project after the Anthology undertaking. Harrison's final TV appearance was a VH-1 record promotion special that was filmed in May 1997. Soon later, Harrison received a diagnosis of throat cancer; he had radiotherapy, which was regarded to be an effective treatment at the time. He publicly attributed the ailment to years of smoking.

Harrison gave a brief rendition of Carl Perkins' song "Your True Love" at the funeral he attended in Jackson, Tennessee, in January 1998. He successfully defended the Beatles at London's High Court in their attempt to take back recordings of a 1962 appearance by the group at Hamburg's Star Club. He was the former Beatles member who was most involved in promoting the release of their 1968 animated film Yellow Submarine the following year.

Harrison and his wife Olivia were attacked at their Friar Park home on December 30, 1999. A kitchen knife attack by Michael Abram, a paranoid schizophrenia sufferer who was 34 years old, punctured a lung and injured Harrison before his wife repeatedly struck the attacker with a fireplace poker and a lamp to render him unconscious. Harrison said, "I felt worn out and could feel the strength leaving me," in a later statement. "I recall feeling a thrust to my chest. My mouth was dripping with blood, and I could hear my lung exhale. I thought I had been stabbed to death."

Harrison was hospitalized after the attack with more than 40 stab wounds, and doctors had to remove a portion of his punctured lung. Soon after, he made the following statement about his attacker: "He wasn't a burglar, and he most definitely wasn't auditioning for the Traveling Wilburys. The historical, spiritual, and groovy Indian figure Adi Shankara once said, "Life is fragile like a raindrop on a lotus leaf." "Furthermore, you better believe it."

Abram said, "If I could turn back the clock, I would give anything not to have done what I did in attacking George Harrison, but looking back on it now, I have come to understand that I was at the time not in control of my actions," after being released from a mental hospital in 2002 after spending less than three years in state custody. "The Harrison family might be able to accept my apologies, I can only hope," he apologetically stated.

Harrison's family understated his injuries from the break-in in their statements to the media. Because Harrison had previously appeared to be in good health, those in his social circle assumed that the attack had altered him and was the cause of his cancer returning. Harrison underwent surgery to remove a malignant growth from one of his lungs in May 2001, and in July it was reported that he was receiving treatment for a brain tumor at a hospital in Switzerland. While in Switzerland, Starr visited him but had to cut short his stay to travel to Boston, where his daughter was undergoing emergency brain surgery. Harrison, who was very weak, quipped: "Do you want me to come with you?"

His non-small cell lung cancer, which had spread to his brain, was treated with radiotherapy at Staten Island University Hospital in New York City in November 2001. When the news was made open to everyone, Harrison lamented his doctor's breach of privacy, and his estate later claimed damages.

Harrison passed away in a McCartney home on Heather Road in Beverly Hills, Los Angeles, on November 29, 2001. He was 58 years old. Shankar, his wife Sukanya, their daughter Anoushka, Olivia, Dhani, and Hare Krishna devotees Shyamasundar Das and Mukunda Goswami, who sang passages from the Bhagavad Gita, were all present when he passed away. Olivia and Dhani quoted him as saying, "Everything else can wait, but the search for God cannot wait and love one another."

His funeral was held at the Self-Realization Fellowship Lake Shrine in Pacific Palisades, California, and he was cremated in Hollywood Forever Cemetery. In a private ceremony, his close family scattered his ashes in the Ganges and Yamuna rivers close to Varanasi, India, following Hindu tradition. In his will, he left almost £100 million.

Brainwashed, Harrison's last studio album was finished by his son Dhani and Jeff Lynne and released posthumously in 2002. The liner notes for the CD contain the following quote from the Bhagavad Gita: "There never was a period when you or I did not exist. Furthermore, there won't be a time in the future when we vanish." Leng sees the media-only song "Stuck Inside a Cloud" as "a uniquely candid reaction to illness and mortality" and notes that it peaked at number 27 on Billboard's Adult Contemporary chart. The UK Singles Chart's highest point for the May 2003 single "Any Road" was number 37. While "Any Road" was up for Best Male Pop Vocal Performance, "Marwa Blues" went on to win the 2004 Grammy Award for Best Pop Instrumental Performance.

<u>ARTISTRY</u>

<u>Guitar Playing</u>

Harrison's guitar playing for the Beatles was versatile and varied. His lead guitar playing was excellent and exemplified the more understated lead guitar style of the early 1960s, despite not being quick or flamboyant. His usage of a capo to shorten the strings on an acoustic guitar, as on the Rubber Soul (1965) album and "Here Comes the Sun," to produce a brilliant, beautiful tone, is one example of his inventive rhythm guitar playing. Harrison, in the opinion of Eric Clapton, was "clearly an innovator" since he "took some elements of R&B, rock, and rockabilly and created something unique." Harrison was regarded as "a guitarist who was never showy but who had an innate, eloquent melodic sense" by Rolling Stone creator Jann Wenner. He provided the song with beautiful playing. Harrison was influenced by the guitar-picking techniques of Chet Atkins and Carl Perkins, which gave many of the Beatles' songs a country music vibe. Chuck Berry was another formative influence, according to him.

Lennon and Harrison co-wrote the blues-inspired instrumental "Cry for a Shadow" in 1961, and Harrison is also credited with writing the song's lead guitar line. The song builds around strange chord voicings and emulates the sound of other English bands like the Shadows. Buddy Holly's influence can be seen in Harrison's wide use of the diatonic scale in his guitar playing, and his fascination with Berry motivated him to write songs using the blues scale and adding a rockabilly vibe in the manner of Perkins. Harrison often used guitar lines that were composed in octaves, as heard in the song "I'll Be on My Way."

A Hard Day's Night's closing chord arpeggios are an example of a section he wrote that used non-resolving tones. By 1964, he had started to establish a definite personal style as a guitarist. He played a Rickenbacker 360/12, an electric guitar with twelve strings, the lower eight of which are tuned in pairs, one octave apart, and the highest four of which are pairs tuned in unison. He used this guitar on this song as well as other songs from the era. His usage of the Rickenbacker on "A Hard Day's Night" contributed to the model's popularity, and the jangly sound became so well-known that Melody Maker referred to it as the Beatles' "secret weapon". Harrison played "I Need You" in 1965 while controlling the volume of his guitar with an expression pedal, producing a syncopated flautando sound with the melody resolving its dissonance through tonal displacements. On "Yes It Is," he employed the same volume-swell technique, giving the song's natural harmonics what Everett called "ghostly articulation."

Harrison brought fresh musical concepts to Revolver in 1966. He performed backward guitar on John Lennon's song "I'm Only Sleeping" and a guitar counter-melody that moved in parallel octaves above Paul McCartney's bass downbeats on "And Your Bird Can Sing." His guitar work on "I Want to Tell You" is an example of how to combine descending chromatic lines with altered chordal colors, and his guitar part on "Lucy in the Sky with Diamonds" from Sgt. Pepper's album mirrors Lennon's vocal lines like how a sarangi player would accompany a khyal singer in a Hindu devotional song.

Harrison's guitar solo from "Old Brown Shoe" was dubbed "stinging and highly Claptonesque" by Everett. Huntley described the tune as "a sizzling rocker with a ferocious... solo" and pointed out two of the composition's key motifs: a bluesy trichord and a diminished triad with roots in A and E. Harrison's "Old Brown Shoe" demo, in Greene's opinion, is "one of the most complex lead guitar solos on any Beatles song."

Harrison's performance on Abbey Road, and especially on "Something," represented a turning point in his growth as a guitarist. The guitar solo for the song demonstrates a wide range of influences, including Clapton's blues guitar style and Indian gamakas. "Something" meanders toward the most memorable of Harrison's guitar solos, according to author and musicologist Kenneth Womack: "A masterpiece in simplicity, it reaches toward the sublime."

Harrison started using slide guitar in his solo work after Delaney Bramlett encouraged him to do so. This allowed him to imitate a variety of traditional Indian instruments, including the sarangi and the dilruba. Harrison's slide guitar solo on John Lennon's "How Do You Sleep?" was characterized by Leng as a break from "the sweet soloist of 'Something,'" and as "rightly famed... one of Harrison's greatest guitar statements." In the words of John Lennon,

"That's the best he's ever fucking played in his life."

The slide guitar work on Harrison's 1982 album Gone Troppo and his 1992 televised rendition of the Cab Calloway song "Between the Devil and the Deep Blue Sea" on the ukulele both exhibit a strong Hawaiian influence. Lavezzoli referred to Harrison's slide playing on the Grammy-winning instrumental "Marwa Blues" (2002) as "yet another demonstration of Harrison's unique slide approach" and compared the melody to an Indian sarod or veena.

Harrison, a fan of George Formby and a member of the Ukulele Society of Great Britain ended "Free as a Bird" with a ukulele solo in Formby's style. He was the honorary president of the George Formby Appreciation Society and performed at a Formby convention in 1991. Harrison contributed to several songs by the Beatles, including "She Said She Said," "Golden Slumbers," "Birthday," and "Honey Pie." Additionally, he contributed bass to some solo albums, including "Faster," "Wake Up My Love," and "Bye Bye Love."

Guitars

Harrison's primary guitar was a Höfner President Acoustic when he first joined the Quarrymen in 1958, but he quickly switched it out for a Höfner Club 40 model. A Czech-made Jolana Futurama/Grazioso solid-body electric guitar served as his first instrument. He mostly played Gretsch models through Vox amplifiers on his early recordings, including a Gretsch Duo Jet that he had acquired and used in 1961 and had posed with on the album cover for Cloud Nine (1987). Additionally, he acquired a Gretsch Tennessean and a Gretsch Country Gentleman, which he used to perform "She Loves You" and accompany the Beatles on The Ed Sullivan Show in 1964. He purchased a Rickenbacker 425 Fireglo in 1963, and the second-ever Rickenbacker 360/12 guitar was obtained by him in 1964. When Harrison first got his hands on a Fender Stratocaster in 1965, he used it to record the Help! an album that February. He also used it later that year to record Rubber Soul, most notably on the song "Nowhere Man."

Harrison and Lennon each bought an Epiphone Casino at the beginning of 1966, which they utilized for Revolver. While recording the album, Harrison also used a Gibson J-160E and a Gibson SG Standard. Later, he gave his Stratocaster a psychedelic makeover, adding the term "Bebopalula" above the pickguard and the nickname "Rocky" for the instrument to the headstock. Throughout his solo career and the 1967 movie Magical Mystery Tour, he used this guitar.

Harrison was given a Gibson Les Paul in July 1968 by Clapton that he dubbed "Lucy" and that had been stripped of its original finish and stained cherry red. He bought a Gibson Jumbo J-200 acoustic guitar around this period, which he later donated to Bob Dylan to use at the Isle of Wight Festival in 1969. Harrison received a Philip Kubicki-made, specially designed Fender Telecaster Rosewood prototype from Fender Musical Instruments Corporation in the latter half of 1968. The "Limited Edition George Harrison Rosewood Telecaster" that Fender issued in August 2017 was based on a Telecaster that Roger Rossmeisl had originally built for Harrison.

Indian Music And The Sitar

Harrison was introduced to Indian classical music and the sitar master Ravi Shankar's work by his friend David Crosby of the Byrds during the Beatles' American tour in August 1965. According to Harrison, Shankar was "the first person who ever impressed me in my life... and he was the only person who didn't try to impress me." Harrison became engrossed with Indian music and developed a fascination with the sitar.

Harrison's use of the sitar in the Beatles' song "Norwegian Wood" allegedly "opened the floodgates for Indian instrumentation in rock music, sparking what Shankar would refer to as 'The Great Sitar Explosion' of 1966–1967," according to Lavezzoli. Harrison is acknowledged by Lavezzoli as "the man most responsible for this phenomenon".

Harrison first met Shankar in June 1966 when visiting Mrs. Angadi of the Asian Music Circle. He subsequently begged to be his student and was granted permission. Lavezzoli views Harrison's sitar contribution to "Love You To" as an "astonishing improvement" over "Norwegian Wood" and "the most accomplished performance on sitar by any rock musician" before this encounter. Harrison had already recorded his Revolver tune "Love You To" before this meeting. Harrison left for India on July 6 to purchase a sitar from Rikhi Ram & Sons in New Delhi. After the final Beatles tour in September, he traveled back to India to study the sitar for six weeks with Shankar. He first remained in Bombay until his presence was discovered by followers, at which point he moved to a houseboat on a secluded lake in Kashmir. He also received instruction from Shambhu Das, Shankar's pupil, during this stay.

Harrison studied the guitar until 1968 when he decided to pick it up again after meeting Clapton and Jimi Hendrix in a New York hotel after speaking with Shankar about the need to rediscover his "roots" in music. In Harrison's words, "I decided... I'm not going to be a great sitar player... because I should have started at least fifteen years earlier."

Harrison stayed closely affiliated with the genre and occasionally used Indian instruments on his solo projects. In Lavezzoli's list of the three rock musicians who have "mainstream exposure to non-Western kinds of music, or the concept of "world music," he is grouped with Paul Simon and Peter Gabriel.

Songwriting

In August 1963, while ill and lying in a hotel bed in Bournemouth, Harrison wrote his first song, "Don't Bother Me," as "an exercise to see if I could write a song," as he recalled. His songwriting skills developed throughout the Beatles' existence, but it wasn't until close to the band's dissolution that Lennon, McCartney, and producer George Martin gave his work their full respect. "Up until this year, our songs have been better than George's," McCartney said to Lennon in 1969. His tunes this year are at least on par with ours in quality. Harrison frequently struggled to convince the band to record his tunes. Harrison wrote at least two songs for every Beatles album released after 1965; Revolver is regarded by Inglis as "the album on which Harrison came of age as a songwriter" because it included three of his songs.

Harrison showed an interest in exotic tones that later led to his appreciation of Indian music by writing the chord arrangement for "Don't Bother Me" nearly solely in the Dorian mode. The latter proved to have a significant impact on his composition and helped him stand out among the Beatles. Harrison's willingness to experiment with different sounds and textures, according to Rolling Stone's Mikal Gilmore, "opened up new directions for his rock & roll compositions. In contrast to the avant-garde characteristics that Lennon and McCartney appropriated from the music of Karlheinz Stockhausen, Luciano Berio, Edgard Varèse, and Igor Stravinsky, his use of dissonance in "Taxman" and "I Want to Tell You" was innovative in popular music.

Author Gerry Farrell described the 1967 Harrison song "Within You Without You" as a "quintessential fusion of pop and Indian music," claiming that Harrison had invented a "new form." Harrison's best song, in Lennon's opinion: "His mind and his music are clear. His natural talent allowed him to put that sound together."

Harrison adopted the Karnatak discipline of Indian music in his subsequent entirely Indian song, "The Inner Light," as opposed to the Hindustani style he had employed in "Love You To" and "Within You Without You." In a 1997 essay, Farrell noted that the Beatles' "Indian" compositions, such as "Blue Jay Way" and "The Inner Light," continue to stand as the most creative and commercially successful instances of this type of fusion. This is a testament to Harrison's true connection with Indian music.

A classic and "an intensely moving romantic ballad that would challenge 'Yesterday' and 'Michelle' as one of the most recognizable songs they ever produced," according to Beatles biographer Bob Spitz, was "Something."

Inglis saw Abbey Road as a turning point in Harrison's growth as a musician and composer. He deemed the two songs that Harrison contributed to the album, "Here Comes the Sun " and "Something," to be "exquisite," ranking them on par with all of the Beatles' prior compositions.

Collaborations

Harrison began working with other musicians in 1968. He invited Eric Clapton to play lead guitar on "While My Guitar Gently Weeps" for the 1968 Beatles' White Album and worked with John Barham on his 1968 debut solo album, Wonderwall Music, which also featured contributions from Peter Tork from the Monkees and Clapton once more. He contributed to songs by Tom Scott, Dave Mason, Nicky Hopkins, Alvin Lee, Ronnie Wood, and Billy Preston. Along with others, Dylan, Clapton, Preston, Doris Troy, David Bromberg, Gary Wright, Wood, Jeff Lynne, and Tom Petty contributed to Harrison's songwriting. Harrison produced Apple Records artists Doris Troy, Jackie Lomax, and Billy Preston during the final years of the Beatles.

The song "Badge," which was featured on Cream's 1969 album Goodbye, was co-written by Harrison and Clapton. For contractual reasons, Harrison played rhythm guitar on the song under the alias "L'Angelo Misterioso". He participated in the recording of six tracks for Bob Dylan's album New Morning in May 1970. He co-wrote and/or produced the top 10 songs "It Don't Come Easy", "Back Off Boogaloo", and "Photograph" for Starr between 1971 and 1973. In addition to "How Do You Sleep?" he also contributed a slide guitar solo to "Gimme Some Truth" and a dobro solo to "Crippled Inside" on Imagine, Lennon's 1971 album. He also produced and contributed slide guitar to Badfinger's top 10 smash "Day After Day" and Preston's "I Wrote a Simple Song" in that year. He collaborated with Cheech & Chong on

"Basketball Jones" (1973) and Harry Nilsson on "You're Breakin' My Heart" (1972).

Harrison established Dark Horse Records in 1974 as a platform for musical collaboration. As Apple Records had done for the Beatles, he wanted Dark Horse to act as a creative outlet for artists.

"He's extremely generous, and he backs and supports all kinds of people that you'll never, ever hear of," Eric Idle observed. Ravi Shankar and the band Splinter were the first artists to sign with the new label. The Place I Love, the debut album from Splinter, was produced by Harrison and featured several of his musical compositions. It gave Dark Horse its first success, "Costafine Town." On the label's other debut album, Shankar's Shankar Family & Friends, he also produced and contributed guitar and autoharp. Dark Horse has also signed Attitudes, Henry McCullough, Jiva, and Stairsteps as artists.

Harrison worked with Tom Scott on Scott's 1975 album New York Connection, and in 1981 he contributed the guitar to Mick Fleetwood's song "Walk a Thin Line" from The Visitor. Harrison continued to contribute to Starr's solo career by writing and producing the 1981 US Top 40 smash "Wrack My Brain" and adding guitar overdubs to two tracks on Vertical Man (1998). Harrison and Carl Perkins collaborated on the song "Distance Makes No Difference With Love" in 1996 for Perkins' album Go Cat Go!
Harrison also contributed slide guitar to Bob Dylan's Under the Red Sky album's title track in 1990. He contributed as a guest musician to

the songs "Love Letters" for Bill Wyman's Rhythm Kings and the comeback album Zoom by Jeff Lynne and the Electric Light Orchestra in 2001. Eight weeks before his passing, on October 2, he co-wrote "Horse to the Water," a brand-new song with his son Dhani. On Jools Holland's album Small World, Big Band, it was included.

Production Of Movies And Independent Films

Raga, a documentary by Ravi Shankar, was released in 1971 by Harrison with assistance from Apple Films. Along with Apple manager Allen Klein, he also produced the Concert for Bangladesh movie. He developed the 1973 motion picture Little Malcolm, but the production was shelved due to the legal dispute over the former Beatles cutting off financial relations with Klein.

Peter Sellers introduced Denis O'Brien to Harrison in 1973. The two soon started a business venture together. They established the film production and distribution business HandMade Films in 1978 to make Monty Python's Life of Brian. Their chance to get money came after EMI Films withdrew support at Bernard Delfont's request, the company's senior executive. Idle later referred to Harrison's mortgage on his home as "the most anybody's ever paid for a cinema ticket in history" as a way that he helped finance the making of Life of Brian. In the US, the movie made $21 million at the box office. The Long Good Friday (1980) was the first movie that HandMade Films released, while Time Bandits (1981), which Terry Gilliam and Michael Palin of Monty Python co-wrote, was the first movie the company produced. At the end of the movie, Harrison's brand-new song "Dream Away" was played. Time Bandits became one of HandMade's most well-known and lauded productions; it had a $5 million budget but made $35 million in the US in its first ten weeks of release.

A Private Function (1984), Mona Lisa (1986), Shanghai Surprise (1986), Withnail and I (1987), and How to Get Ahead in Advertising (1989) are just a few of the 23 movies Harrison worked on as executive producer with HandMade. He had cameo cameos in several of these movies, including Shanghai Surprise, where he played a nightclub singer and cut five brand-new songs. Ian Inglis claims that "Harrison's executive role in HandMade Films helped to sustain British cinema at a time of crisis, producing some of the country's most memorable movies of the 1980s."

HandMade's financial status deteriorated due to a string of box office duds in the late 1980s and enormous debt accrued by O'Brien that Harrison guaranteed. The business discontinued operations in 1991, and a

Canadian entity called Paragon Entertainment purchased it three years later. Harrison then sued O'Brien for $25 million for fraud and carelessness, and in 1996, the court awarded him a $11.6 million judgment.

PERSONAL LIFE

Philanthropic Work

Throughout his life, Harrison was active in both political and humanitarian causes. The Beatles participated in anti-Vietnam War demonstrations and supported the civil rights movement in the 1960s. After the 1970 Bhola cyclone and the Bangladesh Liberation War, Harrison advised Ravi Shankar on how to help the people of Bangladesh in early 1971. The quickly composed and recorded song "Bangla Desh" by Harrison became the first charity single in pop music when it was released by Apple Records in late July. To help spread awareness of the issue, he also urged Apple to release Shankar's Joi Bangla EP. Harrison was consulted by Shankar for guidance on organizing a small charity event in the US. Harrison organized the Concert for Bangladesh in response, and it raised more than $240,000. The album and movie releases brought in about $13.5 million, but because Klein neglected to register the event as a UNICEF benefit beforehand, the majority of the money was blocked in an Internal Revenue Service audit for ten years. In honor of their fundraising efforts for Bangladesh, UNICEF presented Harrison, Shankar, and Klein with the "Child Is the Father of Man" award in June 1972 during an annual ceremony.

Harrison started speaking out in favor of Greenpeace and CND in 1980. Along with Friends of the Earth, he also participated in nuclear energy protests and contributed money to the launch of Terry Jones' green magazine

Vole. He assisted in raising awareness of his wife Olivia's Romanian Angel Appeal in 1990 on behalf of the thousands of Romanian children who had been abandoned by the state after communism in Eastern Europe fell. Harrison collaborated with the Traveling Wilburys on the charity single "Nobody's Child" and put together a fundraising album with contributions from other musicians like Clapton, Starr, Elton John, Stevie Wonder, Donovan, and Van Morrison.

It's been said that the groundbreaking Concert for Bangladesh served as a model for the massive rock concerts for good causes that came after, like Live Aid. A cooperative initiative between the Harrison family and the US Fund for UNICEF, the George Harrison Humanitarian Fund for UNICEF seeks to fund initiatives that aid kids affected by humanitarian crises. They gave $450,000 in December 2007 to aid Bangladeshi Cyclone Sidr victims. The first George Harrison Humanitarian Award was given to Ravi Shankar on October 13, 2009, in recognition of his efforts to save the lives of children and his participation in the Concert for Bangladesh.

Hinduism

Harrison began introducing the other Beatles to Indian spirituality and culture by the middle of the 1960s. They encountered Swami Vishnu-devananda, the creator of Sivananda Yoga while filming Help! in the Bahamas, and he handed each of them a signed copy of his book, The Complete Illustrated Book of Yoga. He traveled to India with his first wife, Pattie Boyd, between the conclusion of the final Beatles tour in 1966 and the start of the Sgt Pepper recording sessions. While there, he learned the sitar with Ravi Shankar, interacted with several gurus, and visited numerous holy sites. He traveled to Rishikesh in northern India in 1968 along with the other Beatles to learn meditation with Maharishi Mahesh Yogi.

Harrison's mid-1960s LSD trips acted as a factor for his early conversion to Hinduism. In an interview from 1977, George remembered:

It happened to me in a flash. My first experience with acid simply opened up something inside of me, and I came to many realizations as a result. I already knew them, so I didn't need to memorize them, but it just so happened that that was the key that unlocked the door and let me see them. I wanted to think of the yogis, the Himalayas, and Ravi's music constantly from the moment I first had them.

Harrison, however, ceased using LSD following a negative encounter in San Francisco's Haight-Ashbury district. In The Beatles Anthology, he related:

That moment marked a turning point in my life; I immediately left the drug cult and stopped using the terrible lysergic acid. I had some liquid that was in a small bottle. It appeared to be pieces of old rope when I examined it under a microscope. I believed that I was no longer capable of processing that in my mind.

In the late 1960s, Harrison converted to vegetarianism following the Hindu yoga practice. He continued to be a lifetime supporter of the teachings of Swami Vivekananda and Paramahansa Yogananda—yogis and the authors of Raja Yoga and Autobiography of a Yogi, respectively—after being given many religious materials by Shankar in 1966. He produced the single "Hare Krishna Mantra" in the middle of 1969, which was performed by devotees of the London Radha Krishna Temple. Harrison afterward met A.C. Bhaktivedanta Swami Prabhupada, who he referred to as "my friend" and "my master" and who was "a perfect example of everything he preached" after also assisting the Temple devotees in settling in Britain. Harrison adopted the Hare Krishna way of life, especially the japa-yoga bead singing, and he became a lifelong devotee. He gave the followers his Letchmore Heath mansion in 1972, which is located north of London. Later, it was renamed Bhaktivedanta Manor and turned into a temple.

He once said of other religions:

"All religions are branches of one great tree. Whatever you call Him, as long as you call, it doesn't matter."

He commented on his beliefs:

Krishna had a physical body and was a human. What makes it challenging is the question of why, if he is God, is he engaged in combat on a battlefield. It took me a long time to attempt to understand that, and once more, it was Yogananda's spiritual interpretation of the Bhagavad Gita that finally helped me to understand what it was. Our mental image of Krishna and Arjuna riding in the chariot on the battlefield. The point is that we are experiencing this incarnation, this existence, which is comparable to a battle, while housed in these bodies, which are like a kind of chariot. The body's senses serve as the horses that pull the chariot, and we must regain control of the chariot by regaining control of the reins. Arjuna concludes by pleading with Krishna to steer the chariot: "Please Krishna, you drive the chariot" because, without Christ, Krishna, Buddha, or any other of our spiritual leaders, we will crash our chariot, flip over, and perish on the battlefield. We chant "Hare Krishna, Hare Krishna" to request Krishna to arrive and take control of the chariot for this reason.

According to Inglis, "Harrison's spiritual journey was seen as a serious and important development that reflected popular music's increasing maturity... what he, and the Beatles, had managed to overturn was the paternalistic assumption that popular musicians had no role other than to stand on stage and sing their hit songs."

Relatives And Pursuits

On January 21, 1966, Harrison wed model Pattie Boyd, with McCartney serving as his best man. Boyd, then 19 years old, had been hired to play a schoolgirl in the movie A Hard Day's Night, where they had first encountered each other on the set. George 'playfully' proposed to her during lunch.

Their divorce was finally finalized in 1977 after they separated in 1974. Boyd claimed that George's numerous affairs played a significant role in her decision to dissolve the union. Boyd referred to an affair with Ringo's wife Maureen as "the final straw" in the last infidelity. She said: "George used cocaine excessively, and I think it changed him. It froze his emotions and hardened his heart." She described the final year of their marriage as "fueled by alcohol and cocaine." After that, she moved in with Eric Clapton, and the two eventually were married in 1979.

Harrison wed Olivia Trinidad Arias, a marketing manager for A&M Records and then Dark Horse Records, on September 2nd, 1978. The couple first spoke on the phone while conducting business for Dark Horse, an A&M subsidiary, before finally meeting in person in 1974 at the A&M Records offices in Los Angeles. Dhani Harrison, their only child, was born on August 1 of that year.

Harrison's home in Henley-on-Thames, Friar Park, which served as the backdrop for the album's cover, and the English manor house and gardens where several of his music videos, including "Crackerbox Palace," were shot, were renovated. Ten people were employed by him to care for the 36-acre (15-hectare) garden. In response to the idea that gardening might be a sort of escape, Harrison said,

"Sometimes I feel like I'm actually on the wrong planet, and it's great when I'm in my garden, but the minute I go out the gate I think: 'What the hell am I doing here?'"

I, Me, Mine, his autobiography, is titled "to gardeners everywhere." The book, which talked little about the Beatles and instead concentrated on Harrison's interests, music, and lyrics, was co-written by Harrison with the former Beatles publicist Derek Taylor. Taylor said, "George is not disowning the Beatles... but it was a long time ago and a short part of his life."

Harrison was one of the 100 people who bought the McLaren F1 road car because he had a passion for sports cars and racing. Since he was a small boy, he had accumulated photographs of racing drivers and their vehicles. When he was 12 years old, he went to his first race, the 1955 British Grand Prix at Aintree. He created "Faster" as an homage to Jackie Stewart and Ronnie Peterson, two Formula One racers. The Gunnar Nilsson cancer charity was founded after the Swedish driver passed away from the disease in 1978, and the proceeds from its release went to it. On December 7, 2011, in London, a 1964 Aston Martin DB5 that belonged to Harrison was sold at auction. Harrison had purchased the car brand-new in

George Harrison

January 1965, and an unidentified Beatles collector paid £350,000 for it.

The Beatles' Relationships With One Another

The connections within the band were close for the whole of the Beatles' tenure. The Beatles "spent their lives not living a communal life, but communally living the same life," according to Hunter Davies. Their closest buddies were one another. According to Harrison's ex-wife Pattie Boyd, the Beatles "all belonged to each other" and George "has a lot with the others that I can never know about." Nobody can understand it or even get past it, not even the wives. "We looked out for each other, and we had a lot of fun together," Starr added. We used to stay in the largest hotel suites, which would take up an entire level of the hotel, and the four of us would eventually end up in the shower just to be together. A hotel room here and there, he continued, "there were some really beautiful, caring moments amongst four individuals. It was an incredible intimacy. Four men who cherished one another. The sensation was fairly strong.

According to Lennon, their connection was "one of a young follower and an older guy... he was like a disciple of mine when we started." Later, the two became close because of their LSD encounters and their shared interest in spirituality. After that, their paths diverged dramatically, with Harrison discovering God and Lennon coming to the belief that individuals are the architects of their own life. Harrison praised his former bandmate John Lennon in 1974, saying, "John Lennon is a saint, he's heavy-duty, he's fantastic, and I love him.

He's such a jerk, but that's what makes him so awesome, don't you see?"

After riding the same school bus together, Harrison and McCartney became the first two Beatles to meet. They frequently practiced and learned new guitar chords together. McCartney claimed that when on tour, he and Harrison frequently shared a bedroom. Harrison has been referred to Paul McCartney as his "baby brother". Harrison said: "McCartney ruined me as a guitar player" in a 1974 BBC radio interview with Alan Freeman. Harrison, though, said in the same interview, "I just know that whatever we've been through, there's always been something that's tied us together." Harrison and McCartney relationship, which both men acknowledged frequently irritated each other, was perhaps the biggest barrier to a

Beatles reunion after John Lennon's passing. "Even to the end of George's days, theirs was a volatile relationship," said Rodriguez. When asked if Paul "pisses you off" in a Yahoo! online conversation in February 2001, Harrison responded, "Scan not a buddy with a microscopic glass -- You know his shortcomings -- Afterward, let his flaws go (Victorian era proverb). Although I'm sure there are enough things about me that irritate him, I believe we have matured enough to acknowledge how adorable we both are.

<u>LEGACY</u>

Harrison and the other Beatles received the title of Members of the Order of the British Empire (MBE) in June 1965. The Queen presented them with their insignia during an investiture on October 26 at Buckingham Palace. The Beatles won an Academy Award in 1971 for the Best Original Song Score for the motion picture Let It Be. He also has a flower variety called the Dahlia named after him, as well as the minor planet 4149 Harrison, which was found in 1984. He was the inaugural recipient of the Billboard Century Award, which is given to musicians for major bodies of work, in December 1992. The honor acknowledged Harrison for playing a "critical role in laying the foundation for the modern concept of world music" and for "advancing society's understanding of the spiritual and altruistic power of popular music." He was voted 11th among the "100 Greatest Guitarists of All Time" by Rolling Stone magazine. The same magazine also ranked him 65th among the "100 greatest songwriters of all time."

The Concert for George was held at the Royal Albert Hall in 2002, one year after his passing. The concert was organized by Eric Clapton, and several of Harrison's friends and musical partners, including McCartney and Starr, performed at it. Monty Python's "Lumberjack Song" performers included Eric Idle, who referred to Harrison as "one of the few morally good people that rock and roll has produced". The Material World Charitable Foundation, Harrison's charity, received the concert's proceeds.

By his former bandmates Lynne and Petty, Harrison was posthumously inducted into the Rock and Roll Hall of Fame as a solo artist in 2004. For the Concert for Bangladesh, Harrison was inducted into the Madison Square Garden Walk of Fame in 2006. Harrison received a star on the Hollywood Walk of Fame in front of the Capitol Records Building on April 14, 2009, thanks to the Hollywood Chamber of Commerce. When the star was unveiled, McCartney, Lynne, and Petty were in attendance. At the ceremony, speeches were given by Olivia Harrison, Tom Hanks, and Idle, as well as Harrison's son Dhani, who chanted the Hare Krishna mantra.

Martin Scorsese's documentary, George Harrison: Living in the Material World, was released in October 2011. Interviews with Starr, Clapton, McCartney, Keltner, Astrid Kirchherr, Olivia and Dhani Harrison, Klaus Voormann, Terry Gilliam, and others are included in the movie.

At the Grammy Awards in February 2015, Harrison received a posthumous Grammy Lifetime Achievement Award from The Recording Academy.

Harrison became the first Beatle to travel to the United States in 1963 when he stopped by Benton, Illinois, to meet his sister, according to a memorial erected by the Illinois State Historical Society.

A mural installation made by artist John Cerney was unveiled in the town of Harrison in 2017.

George Harrison

There are many statues of Harrison throughout the world, including three in his hometown of Liverpool and a bust honoring Harrison's contributions to Bangladeshi culture in Dhaka, Bangladesh's Shadhinotar Shagram Triangle Sculpture Garden.

Made in United States
Troutdale, OR
11/08/2023